BUTTONS
the FAMOUS GOAT

by

Sharon Smith

To order additional copies of this book, contact:
Xlibris
1-888-795-4274
www.Xlibris.com
Orders@Xlibris.com

Dedication

I dedicate this book to my four grandchildren Ashlee, Krese, Krosbi, and Kutter, and also my great grandchildren Ryder, River, and Rhett. You have demonstrated your love for my animals and especially my goats. I love you all. This book is for you. *Nana*

Chapter 1

This is a true story about a little goat that was born on our farm on April fool's Day. We have had many baby goats born here, but this baby was a special goat.

Granddad and I live on a farm in southwest Oklahoma. Life on the farm is a wonderful life to live. We raise peanuts, cotton, wheat, and GOATS.

There are about sixty or more goats here. Last week we took 40 of the goats to the sale. When our Nanny goats have babies we raise them and sell only the Billy goats. Billy goats are boys. We keep all the Nannies which are girls. All baby goats are called Kids. This is the way our goat herd grows, by having more babies. We keep only one big Billy goat, which is the daddy to all the babies.

One evening late I went out to the barn to check the goats. To my surprise there was a Nanny goat having a baby. I watched to make sure everything was fine with her. She had two big Billy goats. I wondered if she had enough milk for them. This was her first time to have a baby and she was having twins. She licked and licked and cleaned them up, so they would be warm and dry, and then they started nursing her. Babies need to nurse the mother as soon as they can to survive.

Ever thing seemed just fine; I went into the house for a while. At bedtime I decided to go back to the barn and check on the mother and her two sweet babies. She was doing well and her babies were nursing. I left the goats and went back to the house. It was bedtime and Granddad and I had a busy day tomorrow.

Later I kept thinking about the babies and could not sleep. I felt like something was wrong so I got dressed and went out again to check on the mother and her two new babies. When I got out to the barn, she was trying to have another baby. *What another baby! How is she going to raise three babies?*

She had her baby and it was a tiny little girl. Watching and waiting for a long time to see that the Nanny and her babies were doing fine. I had to make sure the tiny little girl could nurse her mother. The baby was so much smaller than the two Billy's. She licked and licked her new baby until it was almost dry.

This is the way the Nanny bonds with her Kids. The mother learns the smell of her babies and she can always tell if that is her baby, when there are a lot of other babies around.

The two big Billy goats kept nursing and pushed the new baby out of the way. I picked up the new little girl, putting her under her mother. Hoping she would latch on and nurse her mother. *I think she got a little milk.* The two older ones kept pushing her away.

I knew the little goat would not survive if I left her with her mother and two big brothers. But I wanted the Nanny to take care and bond with her. The baby has to nurse her mother or she would not live.

Maybe if I would leave them alone the Nanny would bond with her and let her nurse. *If the brothers got full and went to sleep, then the little one could nurse the Nanny I thought.* I went back into the house for the night again.

Chapter 2

The next morning I got up early and started packing our suitcases. We were going to the city. Granddad had several days of important meetings he needed to attend. I always go with him when I can.

I thought I better go check on the goats before we left. Back out to the barn I went. Seeing the mother and her two big babies, I did not see the little girl? I looked around and found her all by herself in the corner. She was hungry, cold, and crying. I knew the Nanny did not bond with her because of the two big Billy goats nursing during night. The baby was hungry and cold. She was too small and the bigger goats were too strong for her to be around. *What am I going to do?* She will die if I don't take her in the house and warm her up. She is too sweet to just leave her here; hoping the Nanny would take care of her. The Nanny did not have enough milk for three babies and the Billy's were too big and strong for the little girl to be able to nurse.

I took her to the house, away from the Nanny and two Billy's. She needed to get warm and she needed some milk. When I got inside, I wrapped her up in a warm towel and put her in a little box, I hoped she would survive. Then I mixed up a special formula, I use for baby goats. Putting the formula into a little bottle hoping she would was strong enough to nurse. Sometimes the babies are too weak to nurse, I had to try. She was the prettiest baby goat we have ever had. Her marking and color were so different from the others. The Billy's were white with dark brown heads.

She has two brown spots on her back with a black strip down the center of the spots. Her head is white with two little brown spots that looked like tiny bows above her ears. All four legs are golden with a dark black stripe down the front; it looked like she was wearing fuzzy little boots. Her mouth and lips are dark, as if she was smiling and a little black nose. Her eyes were so cute also. She has black stripes above her eyes like long eyelashes. *I think she will be a keeper if I can keep her alive.*

Ok it is time to try and see if she will nurse. Sometimes I have to force the babies to nurse, but not her. She was so hungry and started nursing at once. She loved the formula and nursed most of the bottle. When she finished, her tummy was full and she was warm and happy. I loved on her and put her back into the little box. She curled up on her towel went to sleep. What a site, so sweet and little.

Chapter 3

Granddad came in and asked "What you were going to do with the baby goat?"

"We need to leave for my meetings, right away."

"We can take her with us!" I said.

"With us?" Granddad said.

"Yes, she cannot live without someone feeding her." I said.

Granddad knew we had to take her if she was going to live. So He found a small cat carrier in the storage room. I packed up towels, a bottle, and put the formula in a small ice chest and we were ready to go to the big city.

I placed towels the carrier and put her inside. She lay down and just looked out the carrier door.

Granddad carried her out to the truck. He flipped the back seat up and placed the carrier on the floor. We loaded the truck with our suitcase and all of baby goat things. We were off to the big city and the baby goat was just a few hours old.

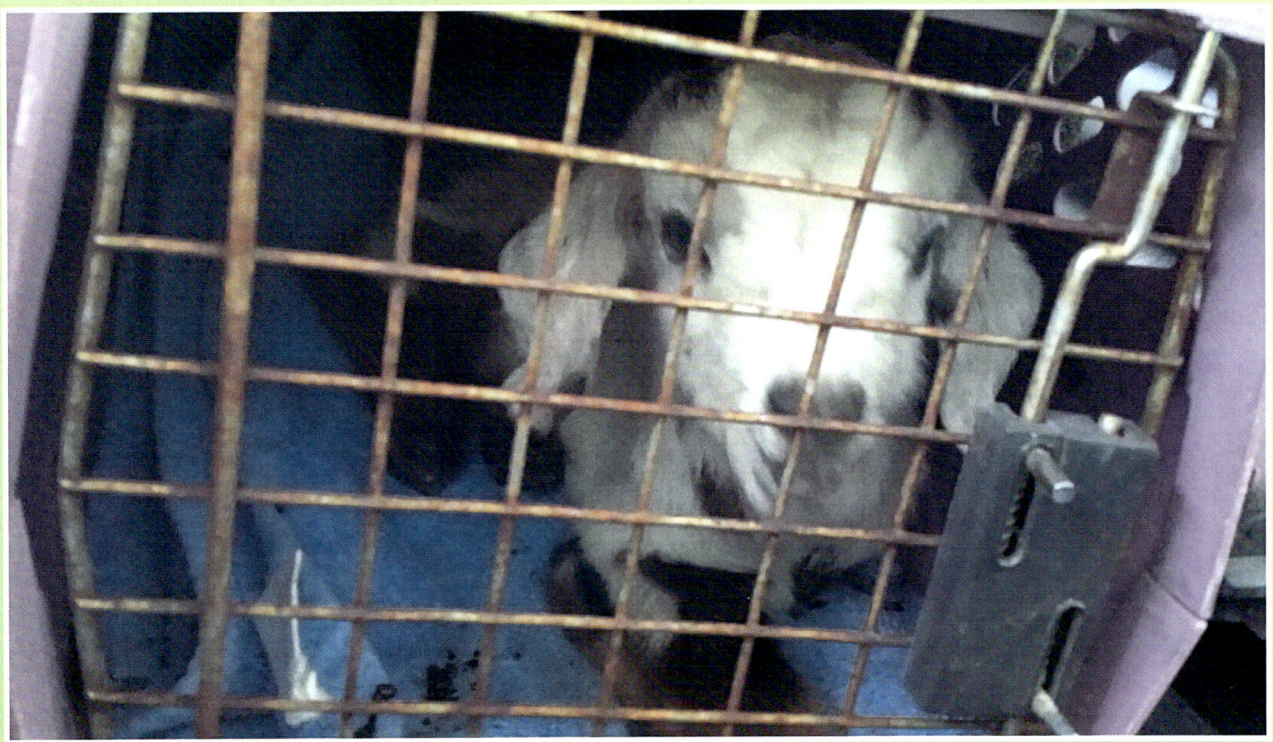

On our way, I called my granddaughter, Krosbi, to tell her about the adventure we were on with a baby goat. She has heard many stories about our goats and bottle feeding them. But not a story likes this.

Krosbi always names our little Nanny goats. We don't name the Billy's; these are the ones we sell.

She laughed about a goat going to the city for three days. I told her the story about the baby goat and how she was born on April 1st, April fool's day. "Shall we call her APRIL?" I said. "I'll send you a picture on the phone so you can see her."

Krosbi called back and said "*Nana,* she is as cute as a button!" "Can we call her Buttons?" "Yes that is a cute name for her" I said.

So that is how "Buttons" got her name!

Buttons started crying she was hungry. We stopped at a restaurant to get a cup of hot water. I put her bottle of special milk into the cup of hot water to warm it. Granddad got Buttons out of the carrier and wrapped her up in a green towel to give her to me. She was so hungry. I gave her the bottle. She nursed it so good. Buttons is learning how to take the bottle. I am so proud she can nurse it.

Away we went down the interstate highway, Buttons nursing her bottle in my lap in the front seat of our truck. I know people wondered as we passed them, *"Was that a goat in that truck?"* We laughed. It did look funny.

After she finished her bottle, I held her as she looked out the window. Then Buttons went to sleep in my arms.

Chapter 4

We arrived at the hotel. Granddad said "How are you going to get that goat in the room?"

"I have been thinking about that." I said. "I can wrap Buttons up in a towel and put your coat over her." "But we will need to hurry to the elevator before she makes any noise."

Granddad checked in for us and got the luggage cart. We loaded the cart with our luggage and Buttons box and her luggage full of formula and towels. I wrapped her up and we were on our way to sneak into the hotel with Buttons.

Pushing the cart, Granddad hurried along, while I went as fast as I could to the elevator. We made it past the front desk and in the elevator to the third floor.

Buttons did not make any noise. I had my finger in her mouth so she could suck it. Granddad opened the door to our room and rolled the cart in. I put Buttons down and she just jumped around. She was so glad to be out of the carrier to play.

I unpacked Buttons things and fixed her little box with towels inside to be soft for her. She had another bottle of milk and went to sleep in her box.

When a Nanny goat is going to graze, she will hide her babies in the weeds or grass to protect them from predators. I guess that is why she was so quite. It is just normal for her to be quite when I put her in her box. She thought she was hid. In a way she was, hid in the hotel room.

By then Granddad was hungry. "Where do you want to go to eat?" "And what are you going to do with that goat?" He said.

"I think I will leave her here" I said. "No one will be coming into the room. I'll leave the TV on for noise. Maybe she will think we are still here. People could not hear her if she woke up and made a noise. They will think it is the TV."

We went out to eat and came back to the hotel.

As we came back in our room, Buttons was just waking up.

I took her out of her box to play. She was so excited, smelling everything, running, and jumping. It was so funny watching her explore. The orange carpet was so soft on her little hoofs and she loved it. But the tile was another thing. It was so slick she did the splits on the tile and fell on her face.

It was so funny. Having a goat in your hotel room is going to be fun.

Granddad went down stairs to visit his friends, while I stayed with Buttons.

Buttons and I watched TV together. I held her in her blue towel all warm and happy. What a day; this goat is not even a day old and staying in a fancy hotel.

I had to tell my friends about Buttons, so I started posting on Facebook about her. There were so many responses and comments about her. Everyone wanted to know what was going on with Buttons. I posted pictures of her in the hotel and wrote comments about her. She is known from Oklahoma to Florida to Illinois to Arizona. What a goat it was so funny hearing what people said and they wanted to know more about her. I knew she was going to be a special goat when I first saw her.

At bed time I fixed her bottle again and she enjoyed it. Then back in her little box she went for the night. Buttons was tired she slept all night long.

Chapter 5

The next day we were going to a funeral. I could not leave her alone, in her box while we were gone. The maid would come in to clean our room. So, yes Buttons went to the funeral. Of course I could not take her in, so I left her in the carrier with the windows open. It was a cool day.

While I was inside I told my friends about Buttons and our adventure. Someone said "I saw that on Facebook. Is she with you?" "Yes, she is" I said. "Would you like to see her?"

Who would have thought I have a celebrity goat. Several people wanted to see the baby goat, which was only one day old.

We went outside after the funeral and took Buttons out of the carrier. They held her and loved on her. Thinking she was so cute, they were amazed how small she was. I guess they did not know what a baby goat looked like, by the way they acted. It was funny how they wanted to take her home with them, as if she was a puppy, not a goat. I told them Buttons will grow up to be a big goat. They were thinking she would stay small.

Who would have thought this little goat has traveled over one hundred and thirty miles, living in a fancy hotel, and has attended a funeral? What a life this little goat has and we still have two more days to stay in the hotel.

Now to sneak her back in the hotel. It is easy to go out of the hotel. There is a back door to go out, but you cannot come in it. You can only go in the front door of the hotel by the front desk where people are standing.

Here I go again; covering her up with a towel and coat like before, only this time she would not let me stick my finger in her mouth. She wanted to make her goat noise. So I had to hold her mouth closed and talk loud to Granddad to cover up her *"Baaaa"* sound. The look on Granddads face; he knew we were going to be caught.

We made it again to the elevator and back into our room. Boy, this is getting harder and harder to slip this goat into the hotel. I am glad we are not staying here a week.

Time to feed Buttons again. Granddad played with her while I fixed her bottle. It is funny when I look in the little refrigerator, and all I see is goat's milk and two cans of orange pop for Granddad. I filled her bottle and warmed it. She was ready and hungry. Buttons went to sleep in her little box again.

You know, a baby goat is easy to take care of if we could stay in the room all day. But we need to do other things. So we were in and out of our room with Buttons several times.

Chapter 6

The next day Granddad went to his meetings again. Buttons and I stayed in the room all day. I read and watched TV. Buttons kept trying to get on the bed, but she was too little. I leaned down and picked her up. She loved to be on the bed and snuggled next to me and she went to sleep. That is what baby goats do, they lay next to their mother to keep warm and secure. *I guess I am a Nanny! Hum mm!!! My grandchildren call me Nana!*

Granddad came back into the room and saw us sleeping. He could not believe what he was looking at, a goat in the bed sleeping with me. Of course Buttons woke up and was glad to see him. She tried to hop off the bed to greet him, but fell to the floor. Granddad picked her up and loved on her. She was just fine.

Time to go out and eat dinner again, I got dressed and then put Buttons in her box. She went to sleep with the TV on again.

Granddad and I ate and went to a movie. We were gone several hours. When we got back Buttons was still asleep in her box. I took her out to play and exercise while I make her bottle. She drank the whole bottle. Back to her box for the night, with a full tummy, what a life for a baby goat.

The next day was the day we were to go home.

I packed up everything while Granddad was attending his meeting. When he came in I was ready to leave.

Now, to go out the back door with Buttons, for the last time hoping no one sees us. Granddad put everything in the truck and I was on my way to slip out the back door. As I was going down the hall Buttons made a loud sound. *"Baaaaaa"* I forgot to put my hand over her mouth. There was a man who worked in the hotel coming through the door and herd Buttons. He said '"is that a bird, you have?" I was so shocked all I could say is "yes" and rushed out the door. *We made it!* I put Buttons in the carrier on her towel. I jumped in the truck laughing and telling Granddad about this man who thought Buttons was a bird.

We drove back home to southwest Oklahoma. Buttons slept all the way. Granddad and I talked and laughed about our trip to the city with Buttons. We had a good time with her. She was becoming a special goat in our life.

Chapter 7

When we got home, I put Buttons down on the ground to meet her new friend Mindy our dog.

Buttons was too little to live with the goats outside without a Nanny to protect and feed her. She had to live with us until she was bigger.

Granddad went out to our storage and found a dog crate. I had to have something for Buttons to stay in. She could not live in our house without a crate. It was too cold outside at night for her to stay out there alone. I placed her crate in the back den. Putting clean towels on one end and puppy pads on the other end of the crate; she was ready for her new home. I placed a green blanket over the top of her crate, so she would feel secure and warm.

I wanted to check the goats, so Buttons and I went out back to the goat pen to see how her big brothers and mother were doing. When Buttons walked into the pen her mother looked and smelled of her. She did not smell like her mother, so her mother walked away. When I saw that I knew she was a goat who could not live in the goat pen. Buttons was still so small, compared to her big brothers and all of the other goats. I needed to take special care of her.

There is a pen out back where we have raised gunnies; it also has a dog house inside the pen. This will be Buttons new home, a place she can play during the day. She will have her own goat house filled with straw. I also put a pan of water in the pen for her. But at night she will come into the house to sleep in her crate.

Granddad went to the coffee shop, to catch up on all the news. When he walked into the shop, one of the guys said, "How is Buttons?" Granddad was shocked they knew about Buttons. The guy laughed and told Granddad about Buttons being on Facebook. He said everyone has enjoyed the stories about Buttons. I even had a friend who wanted to baby set Buttons if I needed it.

Chapter 8

One day we were going to Enid to watch the grandkids play ball. We were going to spend the night there. I ask my friend Diana if she really wanting to keep Buttons over night? She said "Yes I would love too."

Now this little goat has her own baby sitter! Or should I say Kid sitter.

Diana would text me and sends me pictures of Buttons. The cutest picture was, Diana holding her in a green towel watching television with a caption saying, "Oh hey mom I'm just Chill 'in and watching *TV.*" I don't know about this baby sitter, she is spoiling Buttons rotten.

Every morning as soon as I get up I feed Buttons. Then around three I feed her again. When night time comes I bring her into the house for another bottle. She spends the night in her crate. I did this every day for a month. As she got older I would let her follow me to the goat pens. I wanted her to know she was a goat. She really did not like being with the goats. They all had to smell of her and push her. *It was too dirty out there. She liked to live with us.*

But one day I thought I will leave her out there and sneak away back to the house. I would go out to check on her every now and then. She could not get hurt she was still too little. She stayed about one hour out there, and then I went out to get her.

The next day I was going to do the same thing. She followed me to the gate and stopped. She would not move, as if to say "I'm not going out there again."

I laughed at her and picked her up and away we went to the goat pen. I stayed out there for ten minutes then I would sneak away again. When I was going through the second gate I saw this white steak run pass me. It was Buttons. She had crawled through the fence and came running to the house. I took her back and we did it again. I tried it again and this time I made it to the house without her. I was in the house about thirty minutes when I heard someone knocking on the door. I opened the door and who do you think was there? Yes Buttons. She was hitting the door with her head, as if to tell me "I'm back!"

Chapter 9

Buttons is one month old now. She is staying outside at night in her pen, if the weather is warm. One morning I took her a new bottle of milk. Her ears perked up as if to say, *a new pink bottle?* She is so funny.

The next day Buttons had a surprise for me. She looked straight up in my face smiling like she wanted to tell me something.

Look Momma I have little buttons on my head. I looked sure enough she was getting her horns.

It was Easter weekend and all the grand kids were coming in for the big day. Everyone wanted to meet Buttons the Facebook celebrity.

We all went to church together. There were sixteen here for lunch and we had a great time. Coloring eggs was a hit at "Nana's". We always have fun doing that.

I planned a big Easter egg hunt with all the grandkids. Buttons had to stay in her pen. I did not want her to find all the eggs and try to eat them, silly goat.

Krosbi met Buttons and just loved her. Kutter had to feed her the bottle, and Krese wanted to take her home. Buttons made a hit with the family. Ryder, River, and Rhett are my great grandsons. They come to the farm often to play. All of the children are great friends with Buttons. River is seventeen months old and calls Buttons *Butt*. He will go outside and holler *Butt – Butt – Butt* until Buttons comes to the fence. She wants to be petted.

Chapter 10

On our farm we have a lot of cats. Some are cats with names and some are barn cats without names. We also have two dogs. Mindy, a sheltie and Wasilla, a Great Pyrenees. Wasilla guards our goats from predators. She lays in the yard and watch Buttons to protect her.

Buttons is getting bigger now. She stays in the yard to graze during the day.

One day she came to the front porch and lay in Mindy's bed. Mindy looked in the door as if she wanted the goat out of her bed. I think Mindy may be jealous.

The end of school will be soon, Granddad and I plan to take Krese, Krosbi, and Kutter on a trip to the cabin. I need to get my Kid sitter for Buttons again. Diana will keep Buttons for about week. I will pack her formula, bottles, and oats.

Button is eating oats now after she drinks her bottle. It is just like taking a child to stay with a friend. No wonder she thinks she is human.

Diana will keep Buttons for six days. Buttons loves to stay at her house. She plays with the sheep and dogs. Diana has a swimming pool which Buttons enjoys walking around and looking down at the water to see herself. She is such a funny goat. She also climbs on her patio furniture.

Diana husband told me she would take Buttons in the house to watch Thunder basketball on TV. Buttons and Diana are big Thunder fans. It would not surprise me if they didn't have matching Thunder shirts. They are going to miss each other when I wean Buttons. She will start living with the goats. No more Thunder games.

Chapter 11

Buttons is two months old now. There is going to be a big change in her life. She will be getting one bottle a day for a week and then I will wean her away from the bottle.

Granddad moved the goats closer to the house to graze on the weeds that had grown from our rain. We got five inches of rain and the weeds are growing fast.

I opened the gate for the goats to go out to the new pen; they just ran as fast as they could, so happy to eat fresh green food. Now is the time to try to get Buttons to stay with the goats. Buttons will be closer to the house. Maybe she will think she is in the yard.

I took Buttons out to the creep feeder that is full of oats. A creep feeder is for the baby goats only. The big goats cannot go through the bars, only little ones can crawl threw to eat oats. Leaving her there to eat, I went out the gate. But not alone, there was Buttons racing around me and through the gate. This is not going to be as easy as I thought.

Back we went. This time I walked all around the goats with her. She started playing with the other kids, forgetting about me. I hurried out the gate and went in the house. As I watched out the window I saw Granny (our old goat) butting Buttons. She ran over to Karmel (my last bottle baby). Karmel butted Buttons too. Then she ran over and started playing all alone. I know this is sad but that is how goats let the kids know who the boss is.

When I looked out again there was Buttons playing with the other Kids and then she started grazing. It has been five hours now and she has not slipped through the fence. Maybe this is going to be easy to wean her.

It is June now and Buttons is not taking a bottle. She is eating her oats and weeds. Buttons is growing so fast now. She is almost as big as the other baby goats her age.

I still keep her in her own pen at night and with the goats during the day. She hollers *BAAA* every time I go outside or drive up in the driveway. She is always looking for me. We have a routine every day. I feed her oats then put her in with the goats. At bed time I feed her oats again and she goes in her little house to sleep. It will be several months before she can sleep with the goats because she does not have a mother to sleep next too during the night. But time will come she will just lie next to another goat and sleep in the goat pen.

Chapter 12

It is July and we are going to be gone for five days. I am leaving Buttons with the goats this time. I think she will be just fine. I have someone checking on her and the goats every day.

While we were gone Bryan, our son, called and said Karmel just had a baby girl today. I was so excited to know about Karmel. This is her first baby.

We rushed home to see Karmel and her baby. When we got home we could not find her baby. Karmel was crying and came to me looking me in the face. She was trying to tell me something was wrong. Karmel's baby was lost and she could not find her. She wanted me to help her find it.

We started looking for the little baby, Karmel right with us calling her Kid. Looking everywhere, around the pens, weeds, and even out in the field, we could not find the baby. Karmel went back to the pen for a drink of water. We kept looking. After about two hours we found the baby asleep in some weeds. I picked the baby up and called Karmel. She turned around and came running when she saw me holding her baby. I put it down and Karmel just licked and licked her she was so happy. Buttons came to see what was going on. She saw a baby smaller than her. Karmel butted Buttons, as if to say leave my baby alone.

I called Krosbi to name the new baby girl. She was not home so Kutter her brother wanted to name this one. Kutter is five years old. He wanted to name the baby Sissy. So Sissy is her name.

I cannot believe what a good mother Karmel is. She is also taking care of Buttons now. I think she knows Buttons needs a mother goat. Buttons stays with Karmel and Sissy all the time.

Buttons and Sissy play together and sleep together. I am so happy Buttons has found a friend to be with. Sissy and Buttons are best friends now. They are always together with Karmel.

Buttons has become a goat now. She hangs around with the other goats and is very happy with them. I think it is because Karmel has accepted her as a friend and takes care of her. I don't worry about her now she will be just fine. The other goats are nice to Buttons also. I see her playing with all the other little goats.

Buttons has been a joy to raise and watch her do funny things. She will live on our farm forever; she will grow old here with the other goats. When Buttons gets bigger she will have babies of her own. I will enjoy watching her babies grow. They will remind me of her when she was just a tiny little goat.

Buttons is four months old now. She will always be remembered as the tiny little goat that was on Facebook who traveled to the big city, staying in a hotel and went to a funeral. People still stop me and ask about her.

My famous goat "Buttons."

The End

Edwards Brothers Malloy
Oxnard, CA USA
November 12, 2014